# Nobody's Jackknife

*Poems by*
*Ellen McGrath Smith*

First edition: November 2015
Paperback ISBN 978-0-9910742-8-0
West End Press / P.O. Box 27334 / Albuquerque, New Mexico 87125
For book information, see our website at www.westendpress.org

Book design by Lila Sanchez
Cover art by Patricia Bellan-Gillen, *Recollection/Relocation,* Serigraph with collage, 32" x 38", 2008

*For my mother, Joan (McGrath) Smith,*
*who taught me yoga, love, and language*

# Contents

## IV.

What to do with my arms? They
coil out of my body

like snakes.
They branch & spit.

I want to shake myself
until they fall like withered

roots; until
they bend the right way —

until I fit in them,
or they in me.

I have to lay them down as
carefully as an old wedding dress,

I have to fold them
like the arms of someone dead.

—Toi Derricotte, "Invisible Dreams"

**1.**

# The Locust: A Foundational Narrative

You do not know
where in earth they go
and when
they're coming back,
but when they're here
the world is
*machinale,*
the air is full
of consequence.

❧

It lay there like a father who had worked a double-shift, not dead, but not ready to resume its upright role any time soon. When the graying locust fell from lightning, I learned that the directions and pulls of the earth operated independently of my location. The tree was on a hill behind our house; it was broken by electric teeth, nosed over by a dogged western wind, and even though the center of my drama was that the tree could have smashed our house, it didn't. It was also a bridge between our yard and the Wallaces', waiting for us to make something new of it. It became a pirate ship we rocked — when there were lots of us to rock it — its accidental entropy the only ocean I would know until I was 19. It was "taken away" the way, a few years before, the cat had been "put to sleep." Generations of sapling and young adult locusts struggled up and down our hill, while next door's yard became a forest, something I understood as having to do with the son's involvement in drugs.

❧

I am running down the hill beside the Maronite church, having given myself ultimatums: soldiers are after me, robbers are after me; I'm a saint and some pagans are after me, ready to make me a martyr. Could I endure being burned at the stake? The flames are just words, and I learned to read with such ease that no one can remember my learning. I am running home to dinner, but it has to be more. And although I'm not the naked girl running from my own napalmed skin, we share that puzzling grin below our navels, the grin that, more and more, makes me wonder: Am I really weaker than my brothers? I am running faster than a person ever ran, am running right into a bullet with my forehead. The impact sends its echoes through my skull, and I stop running near the bottom of the hill. No blood. I look around for enemies — my plastic-soled feet throbbing from repeated slaps on the macadam — and see it, on the ground, the bullet, near my foot, still singing a thin bass to the collision. It's winged and near-transparent, more in shock than I am. When I right it, it can't fly away, this tight-wound reel of programmed flight I interrupted. The wings seem manmade, high-tech, and its body's a transistor.

❦

He was a man who couldn't take joy<br>
in children.<br>
They were tiddlywinks spinning into vaultless skies,<br>
unmanned power saws,<br>
brakeless cars. And he had many children.

❦

There is nothing to Google if I wanted to prove my genetics of baseball. If I click on my mother in person, she'll tell me my father pitched semi-pro ball while he was stationed with the Air Force in Kansas City. She'll tell me he might have gone on to the pros. That it stopped somewhere. He's dead, so I can't ask him to show me the chalk lines, the choices, the place where he dropped the ball. With my own equipment, I fill in: heavy drinking, bad temper, low tolerance for frustration. Too much for a gangly right arm to overcome.

I worked hard not to throw like a girl; I could throw far or near with a measure of precision. My shoulders were loose, which can help with expression, extension, finesse — in the way that a pitch is a sentence or song, with beginning and middle and end, yes; but also with rise, stride, some reticence, then the acceptance of landing for better or worse. The times he played catch with me were so rare they were edged with self-consciousness. My brothers, each in turn, approached baseball and got Dad's attention for a time, which was not necessarily a good thing. Those few occasions when he was in the stands at Little League games, he yelled at the coaches, the umpires, the kids (with a special sort of yelling reserved for his own kid). He never came to my softball games, though I did pitch. I had a spinner, and I took the act of pitching very seriously. When I was on the mound, there was a force-field around me of atoms charged with both my hope and my failure.

A good arm. I'd have liked him to tell me I had one.

❦

He laughed so hard he cried
telling my mother about
the boys' invention. They tied
fishing line around the locusts
and were flying them like tiny
buzzing kites. I saw
teardrops in his eyes.
If he could've, he would've
shaken off his shell and torn
down the alley shouting,
                    Let me try!

❦

When I go walking with my mom, we look into so many yards, both of us with a longing we don't have to mention. So many yards know what trees are and how they blend into the overall picture of yards. There are some full of lip-blossomed maples my mother thinks are Japanese. In our house full of boys and men, books are what I have in common with my mother. Books are lady things.

❦

A triple play is a scribble, the seismograph
needle making tight little harsh little angles.
Here are the possible triple-play combinations:
shortstop to third base to second to first, or
more commonly, third snags and steps on his base
before zinging it over to first, who backhands it
to second. Triple plays are more likely when
bases are loaded and runners start running
as soon as it looks like the ball will break through.
I imagine a catcher-to-first-base can happen if,
on a strike-out, ball's dropped, batter runs,
catcher grabs it and steps on home plate,
stops the forced run then whales it to first,
where the runner to second is just getting going
and the runner to first's almost foot-to-the-pad.
I keep score in a notebook covered in stickers,
filled up with clippings and lists of statistics.

There's a pool of grease in the middle of the garage.
A cool rising up from the floor. My bike is broken.
My sleeves are rolled up. I'm a 12 year-old tough guy,
a girl standing here, hands in my back pockets,
trying to think of a way to repair it. My companion,

my transistor radio, is tuned in to the Pirates game;
my emotions break down into innings, at-bats.
I know every catch in the play-by-play voices;
I count RBIs, ERAs, home runs, errors. Upstairs,
my father's watching the same game on TV.

I step outside to spit on an elephant ear.
There are tools on the floor, and I think that,
by spitting, I'll know how to use them.
My bike needs fixed, but I won't ask for help.

## 25. *Salabhásana* One (Plate 60)

Salabhá means a locust. The pose resembles that of a locust resting on the ground, hence the name. In the beginning it is difficult to lift the chest and the legs off the floor, but this becomes easier as the abdominal muscles grow stronger. (B.K.S. Iyengar, *Light on Yoga*)

❦

My mother has a book about yoga,
another book on top of it to keep it open
as she sits on the living room floor
and maneuvers her limbs to match those
of the thin blond-haired girl in the photos.
The book teaches her, and she teaches me.
We make animal shapes with our bodies.

I try it again and again, and cry
because my body fails to hear the brain's
commands. Inert and facedown,
I try it again and again—full locust—
join my hands below my pelvis, push them
down like a lever. Still, my lower body
doesn't rise, which means I cannot fly.

❦

A trick my mother has shown me, a way to help me do the locust until my *abdominal muscles grow stronger*: Clasp hands into a single fist and bury them under my torso to form a kind of lever. This puts the fist right under my pubic bone, which makes me feel ashamed.

❦

If you touch the cartilage of my right ear, you can feel the dent where the rusty fence snagged me. We were using it for a backstop in the baseball field we built on the dump. The boys insist that this was all their project, but this dent proves I was there as well, dragging the powdered orange metal through the vines. We made dugouts, too. I had a pack of stolen cigarettes I kept in one. Sometimes, I'd step out of the house and go down there for a smoke. It never tasted very good, but added height and maybe balls to my macho solitude. The pack lasted a long time. I hid it underneath the boys' contraband *Playboys* full of women who looked like another species altogether. It had ripped a chunk out of my ear, the fencing, and later, when I learned of Van Gogh, I thought, *I know what you mean.*

✳

The way he laughed, my father, at my brothers' wild invention with the locusts!
Like he had never seen them before and was thrilled to discover that they were his.

✳

Another book my mother shared with me: *The Good Earth* by Pearl S. Buck. This writer lived in China, and she won a Nobel Prize.

*"This child of ours is a pretty little maid, even now. Tell me, were the pretty slaves beaten also?"*

*And she answered indifferently, as though it were nothing to her this way or that,*

*"Aye, beaten or carried to a man's bed, as the whim was, and not to one man's only but to any that might desire her that night, and the young lords bickered and bartered with each other for this slave or that and said, 'Then if you tonight, I tomorrow,' and when they were all alike wearied of a slave the men servants bickered and bartered for what the young lords left, and this was before a slave was out of childhood — if she were pretty."*

✳

Face-down and lying on your fist; the king is calling,
you must go and please the king. Very young
and dying on your fist. Tears in your eyes.
Where did you learn about the ways
the kings commanded?

                              What is this shuddering about?

✺

*Let us suppose that God's voice is psychologically equivalent to the
father's, an assumption that is warranted through a thousand
experiences. Thus at the core of the basic situation would be the fact
that the prohibition of feminine experiencing is connected with her
feelings for her father; and that this prohibition, projected to the
father, pushes her into a masculine role. The complete breakdown
would therefore not arise because she loves an enemy of the country,
but because she loves at all.* (Karen Horney, *Feminine Psychology*)

K
is what you put down for a strikeout. One time,
some fans draped a banner at the stadium
consisting of three Ks. It gave me chills when I first saw it,
but all it meant was they were rooting for the pitcher
to retire a whole inning's worth of batters.

I heard Dutch Ryan up the street tell Mrs. Miller,
"I wouldn't cross the street to watch those niggers
play." The day Roberto died, I looked up
at the picture window of his house and tried to burn
my eyes through the smugly drawn drapes.
Later that day, I traced in pencil my old poster of Clemente,
his perfect nose, the sleek column of his *arrogant* neck,
smoothing out the wrinkles in the glossy —
my father'd torn it down and crumpled it, saying
I shouldn't have men like that
on my bedroom wall.

✺

In another fantasy, the kings are strewn throughout the stadium,
indistinguishable from the queens and princes, thousands of
them, paying fans, and the mound you ground against your fist is now a
mound of packed ground. Homing, you lift up one leg,
pull your arm back and hurl the white light toward the open leather fist.
The catcher is a locust crouching there inside the chain link foliage
of Sunday afternoon. Day of the Lord. American Pie. Delivery.

My mother showed me a variation of half-locust:
lift the one extended leg and rest its thigh on the sole
of the foot of the other, bent to be a sawhorse
or step-ladder. Even now, she's the one who says,
*You're making it harder than it needs to be.*

*You're some kind of nympho*, he said, thorax raised above me,
words of love shed at the doorway with the pieces of our clothing,

a blaze of bourbon lighting up the cluttered space between.

I asked him if he meant *eternal teenager*, for if he did,
I could admit to it. The grass was always greener,

and my hind legs tried to match the height of every greener blade.

The difference between a nit and a nymph
is greater than the difference between
a nymph and an adult. The song of the locusts
rises up the shafts of the trees surrounding you.
The song that is like the concession to hay
the grass makes, like the hum in your throat
when you know that you love having this
in your mouth, (though you know that this
isn't real power — in spite of the tears in his eyes
at the end —)


At which point the poem wants to turn back to nature and explain, or
run away from itself and its subject. Of course, they drill deep holes into
the ground. Of course, the hatchlings go in there, and many years go by.
No doubt they are like violins submerged in water.


Summer, when it's under siege.

II.

# The Annunciation
*after the painting by Henry Ossawa Tanner*

There was so much Robe, and all of it weighed,
melted-candlewax drippings of dun-colored
Robe: How on earth could she ever say "no"?

In the crack in the wall, she had seen her own maidenhood,
bloodied yet somehow intact, and the fact that the rug
at her feet buckled there, in the middle, was only more proof

that this life was a series of doings, undoings.

What flag can a teenage girl fly that isn't already translucent,
x-rayed by the sun, its diurnal laws, golden gavels, ramrod
pillars of heat and becoming?  She isn't quite sure,

you can see that. And so men adore her and force
all their women to look up like that and accept
that a "yes" is *pro forma*, and only a "no" carries

weight even greater than all those tan robes. Piled
black crepe in one corner, glowing urns in the other.
Crow's feathers, crone's ash in the shadowy arches

where her mind's gone to live.

## Gin & Tonic

Summer with its Bacchus-head of grape leaves.
Summer with its berry-bloodied grin.
The invisible highwire
from Venus to the moon
mid-June to salmon-sun September.

The power of green aspiration:
onion bulbs, beginner's luck.
The lime-pitched traffic of birds in the morning
on the branches of your nerves,
the cat and the lemony canary,
cellophane laundry hanging out to dry—
moss on white wicker, spiked heels
on wet flagstones, lavender and sweat,
conversational hearts
on the faces lit
by flameless torches.

# Happy Hours

It was 1984 and I worked downtown, in PR. There were a lot of happy hours. I was young. It occurred to me that it might be good, since I was wearing suits to work, to start drinking martinis. There was a bar called Alexander's Graham Bell; I forget now, but maybe it was on Market Square? Every table had an old-fashioned phone, the kind that stood up like a monstrance with one eye, and you could call people up at other tables, as in pick them up. I went with Stacy from Penn State. An intern, close to my age, up and coming. Stacy lived to be professional. I tried to live to be professional, but all of this was boring me. I thought of myself as literary. Still, the suits and Aigner pumps were my own effort. There was a song then by Adam Ant about how you don't drink don't smoke what do you do? And I was starting to do them all. There must have been something *inside*, too, some *innuendo*. It was weird to take the bus home after drinking all night. When I first started getting paychecks, I cashed them. It took over a year for the notion of checking account to dawn on me. I only wanted college back and history classes, carrels of purest reverie and 50-cent drafts in the dive bar downtown where versions of our grandfathers came early, left early and acted, when the moment called for it, like Jackie Gleason or Art Carney, depending upon their chosen masculinity. Pantyhose and air-conditioning. Press kits and media runs. Lions guarding banks. There was a guy I liked but who did not like me back but could tolerate fucking me after a few drinks. That night with Darcy, I saw him on the other side of the bar, sitting there with that phone next to him. His mustache verged on handlebar but at the last it demurred, which made him seem a young Confederate general. I was losing weight with Ex-lax and often had to leave the office in a rush. When we'd leave the bars and head for home on weeknights, there was a sadness to downtown like after a parade; I'm thinking of those very wide brooms the honest truth-pushers must push when all is said and done and we regret confetti. My head tingling on the way to my apartment with the knowledge that I was my father's daughter and there he was sitting on a sofa ten minutes away watching nature shows, sober, why didn't I go over and raise hell the way he did when we were kids? Born from his frothing brain, like Aphrodite. Sometimes he didn't flush and there was a head of foam in the john, so to speak. And white flecks of foam in the corners of his eyes. Oh, how I loved him and I could not stop him from any of this. Another happy hour was at the Library, a discotheque with bookshelves all around. Most of the guys preferred talking to women with hair the color of chicken broth. I could then take out my notebook and write things like, "Flawed blond beauty." Manny made slide shows of the people having fun there and these slide shows strobed the walls around the dance floor; I was never there. And then there was the one in Oxford Centre, at Hillary's. The ultimate yuppie happy hour primarily because there was a patio (new concept in the 80s: the outdoors). Gucci bags were everywhere and men still wearing Aramis, occasionally Obsession. I was standing on my head a real long time, like a martini.          •

# Martini

underpin hosiery    dry cleaning particles
voices declaring the path to promotion
partitions    Post-it notes    skyscraper static

the olive understands

(in a booth holding hands
while the subway forgets its way
—sober squares— home)

thin tower of clarity: olive thinks *should I?*
decisions    pronouncements
briefcases beached against the brass rail

the uniforms loosen    neckties    vestigial tails
nipples muffled    oxford cotton
pumps are weapons    olive severed
from the    tree    this laboratory's

red insides    suspended in verticals of glass
the red dreams steep until    the jacket
standing up and pulling firmly    (make it fit)

                              heads back

## Absinthe

*"Yes,"* said the girl. *"Everything tastes of licorice.*
*Especially all the things you've waited so long for, like absinthe."*
— Ernest Hemingway, "Hills Like White Elephants"

To have waited so long for an
Afternoon Death

To have never ingested true wormwood

To have sat at the edge of a
precipice watching the sun
sliding down all the while holding on
to your very own crumbling horizon

To have swallowed your tongue 'til tomorrow

To have longed for so-long to blossom back into
hello I have missed you more than I can say

To have stayed in one place inside bliss-bower green
inside clouds that were portents of nothing

To eat symbolist flowers plucked
from their evil surroundings

To see stars fill the sky
like the bowl of a spoon
full of holes from your breathing
to heaven from earth

To give birth to the breath
of the moment each moment
while tasting what only the lonely
who love their aloneness can taste.

# Port

The bottom of the day, the bottom of a well
musty with yes and no and maybe not.
But, here, you know where you are
relative to the sky and tomorrow,
that half-shut eye. The depth is cold,
but the width is narrow as a womb,
a coffin, a bed draped in heavy red velvet,
gold tassels on the corners. In this well
like the barrel of a pistol in a gothic novel,
passions take forms—rat-bodied, out of sight,
but nearby, almost welcome when you light
the lantern for as long as you can bear.

Will they eat you when you sleep?
                                    At this point, you don't care.

# How Apart People Are in Time Together

*"I was thinking about time* — he gropes —
*you know how apart people are in time together and apart at the same*
*time* — stops."

—Anne Carson,
*Autobiography of Red*

What happens is the world-grope, where lover A leaves a message
        lover B denies getting, and lover B makes a cold-call, later,
asking *Did you call me? I see you on my caller I.D.* A tree's communication
        with a cactus several thousand miles away could not be thornier,
less tethered to the real (if "real" is where the roots live). Lover A
        is just an echo thrown for lover B's loose bearings. Where
lover A did not, in fact, call the second time, but compensation for
        the real call that had been denied looped in to the periphery
of just when lover A is sure of where she stands. Sheets like open
        hands: again, Anne Carson making Herakles say to Geryon
*Can't you ever just fuck and not think?*—And so, to make the bed,
        but not to make it tight as some monastic trampoline, is what
the doctor orders. In addition to four lush peonies weighing down
        the stems that pushed them into blossom, there is Venus
hiding all the lost domestic cats between her bluegray thighs.
        Lover B becomes George Washington, crossing many rivers
and stroking just enough to get to the dry other side; lover A
        remembers cherry pie and weeps for the loss of her cat.
Tiki torches spell the angles of the next-door balcony, where
        the conversation sounds like a Bukowski poem, but held in
loosely as a Sunday-night functioning drunk. On the peonies,
        ants are running errands. Petal by petal they fall off the globe.
The world-grope is a state of mind that pulls in states like Delaware,
        then just as easily lops them off and flushes them through
Atlantic pipes — abstract lands where beaches grow in season
        and the credit extended for some necessary pleasure
eventually runs out —

## Stout

As in it hits the spot, the spot in which you live, i.e., you live where you are present. When you aren't inside the brown glass beading sweet and bitter of the day condensed—where are you? Forgiven by the skin when caked in mud. A Pilgrim's Progress free pass from the straight and narrow. Hops and hops and hops and hopes like hockey pucks on ice.

Wholesome: good for the eyelashes. Fiber for nursing women. Stout as Stein and squat as boxhedges separating greener grass from just the plain, which has to mean the world is just a bee in your bonnet, a valley of tears, and a dull dry powdery dross.

As in, I spot you; it takes one to know one. As in, if you would rather sit inside that mulchy barrel all night long than be with me: I understand. I wish to God that I could join you caked in mud and full of hops. I wish to God that I could join you.

## Minor Casualty, 2003

Just as she began to walk boldly in daylight,
as she began to hear what, before,
there were laws against hearing
and, listening, walked boldly
past figures in black
who were biting their tongues—
as the swollen hips of buses turned corners,
she dangled her arms like she actually had power
and jangled her keys—metal army—
remembering milk-carton armadas
she'd floated in gutters, a child too devoted
to the mission, too painted in mud
to hike up her jeans by the beltloop.

The father-mechanics amazed her, the way
in the middle of making machinery work,
in the middle of wrenches and drills
and cement—they would hike up their jeans
by the beltloop, remembering their bodies
but never so long that the work went undone.

(Pirates once hid in her pockets, prepared
to invade at her cough, her command,
while nightsticks and whiteness
kept her borders safe from the riots of '68,
and in that safety, she rehearsed a courage
no one wanted or needed —)

Garbage trucks thudding like tanks
through the alley and weeping
their maggoty juice through the canvas,
competing, competing with lilac.

As she marched boldly against the war
wearing postures from imagined wars,
passing cars shot out obscenities, blood
vessels throbbed in unsheathed bayonets,
jonquils bobbed in windowboxes,
bunting—red, white, blue—kept up its blithe
though frightened laughter,
old women dropped their satin scarves
of prayer from robberbaron balconies.

The way satin sipped the light of Easter's death
and resurrection made her stop and stare—
neat green awnings, gentle screen doors, malt-scent
of pushmowers hissing and snapping the small stalks
of lawn; ice cubes and mint in a neighbor's glass tumbler;
an atomizer doubled in a mirror, candies wrapped
in pastel netting, hair ribbons, crisp white-picket
settings; lavender—her mother—the lotion
her mother had very soft skin—

And her swagger slipped off, though she kept on
walking. It pooled on the ground near a curb.
MEN ARE BACK—the headlines claimed;
she hadn't known they'd gone away.
Mechanics fathers firemen soldiers
—a clatter that grew louder:  choppers?
tomahawks? syncopated with loud sun
beyond the sight and strength of anyone.
They do, they fix, they move the earth
around. Bunker busters, shock and awe,
ads celebrating their re-won erections.
They wanted her courage but not her conviction.
The satin scarves twisted, mid-air, into hawks.

## February Was Only Half Over

February was only half over, and so I decided to roll all the change.
I emptied all the tin cans and jars; the bedspread was covered in coins.

I decided to pawn the wedding ring. On the bus after,
I cried, thinking how the jeweler shaped the love-knot out of wax,
then poured the gold over. I paid the light bill with that.

Those rolling tubes ran out, and so I decided to count out the coins,
then stack and wrap units in foil:
> 50 pennies=one half-dollar
> 40 nickels=$2
> 50 dimes=$5
> 40 quarters=$10

Soon after, I would sell the antique dental cabinet.
On the Internet, I pretended I knew what I had.
That took care of half my June expenses.

This was the year the cost of cigarettes spiked.
I bought a rolling machine and spent 2004
rolling pennies, nickels, quarters, dimes, tobacco.

I realized, after rolling coins, that my hands had touched everyone
somehow. Some people soak coins in alcohol first—germs—
but getting sick was the last thing on my mind.
Filling every sleeve with my upright middle finger,
I was getting through the month and touching everyone.

## Rolling Rock Beer

They don't get out much, the horses inside me.
What I wouldn't give to let them out just once a year,
the way the rich Scots-Irish do, up in Ligonier—
groomed and toned to jump and race at Rolling Rock.
They chomp at the bit, day by sober day, while all across the state, beer
distributors and bars are stocked with cold green cans
of pastureland and yeast,
the Loyalhanna boiling down the Laurel Mountains
over the prehistoric cliff where's someone's scrawled:
*If you love something, let it go.*


I once lay back on that cliff while my horses fanned
and ran slipshod over Mellon land, hill and dale.
And I can't help but feel that, somewhere in Westmoreland County,
in the back of a dark bar,
somebody strums on a guitar and sings Rocky Top—
after all that has come and gone, whole decades
later—and it still goes down
like novelty or, at least, the status quo for those who sit and listen,
a cold Rock on the table, fingers at a gallop
on the denim fields of thighs, buzzing neurons doing
their own version of the steeplechase,
following the invisible fox, with a certain formal grace,
all the way to Sunday.

## The Latching-On Song

near my heart there are eyes that can see the wild lights of the inside /
with my head tilted back I could swallow the tail
of the otherwise world

I wet like the cave that hears sun but can harbor the infrared dark
and not die / I might come, I might cry, I am

poised on a perilous peak as the silver wires lash at the hide
of mammalian memory, dumb

with the fullness that opens the mouth not to breathe or to speak
but to interrupt edges

she latched on (lovely coconut head) long ago, when she needed my milk
to survive / the thrill
of a tree plucked of fruit (the limbs shiver) / the tree that remembers
its roots (*I am here*).
even now, I can feel her latch on, latching on, latching into a place
where the red clay
cracks open, the crystal tongues giggle, the blossoms insist.

# First Communion

Every tongue awaits the body.

Every body is a word.

Every word a possibility.

Grant the open wound
its correspondence to
some mystery unshrouded.

Give the heart its place within
the grape-dark midnight sky.

Skull, full of sparkling water.

Joy like a fly trapped in honey
(where its wings were:
a chronic neuralgia).

Each head that crowns
each roseate petal
says it again. Then,
the jagged cry
that means it's alive.

Whole hungry centuries!
Eyes of intelligence
opened and closed!

Lambs in the meadow
each spring.

The tottering legs
of original love.

III.

## Corona: The Apples in Winter

The emotions go somewhere. Like water, they find
their own depth and go somewhere.
The salmon-smudged sunset unravels December
as Saturn comes in to make judgments,
name debts. Sadness not anger
erects the soft fence around everything.
Inside the soft fence are razors embedded,
and love does not know what to do
in the churchyard. She waves at the traffic,
that's all; and the traffic is one long tough
sinew, a cobra bewitched by digestion,
a thigh that remembers each hand
that has stroked it, though none
of those hands is around anymore.

Though none of those hands is around
anymore, one can still see them
waving, descending like birds, wings
spread out to caress. The apples of
so many eyes falling into broad barrels
with frostmetal staves; kisses belying
the fear at the core that the love
will not last. The churchyard protected
by razor blades whispers its vespers
to sleepers whose sinews stretch
fitfully in their aloneness. It whispers
to wave those hands down from the sky.
The children spread their toes and gulp
in the magic with fluttering eyes.

I gulped down the fluttering magic, our lies
with their blue intonations, tragic salt angles
of elbow and crotch, the marzipan whites
of the fingernails, eyes. And bewitched by
digestion, I writhed through the musky tall grasses
and moaned to find something I'd lost.

Love waves against traffic; that's all
in the past, she proclaims through the fumes
and the sunset-tinged mist. Halogen eyes
pick their way through the deepening dark.
It is mild for December. The mulch still has flavor
and I still digest, writhe to leave you behind
and to try to adjust to aloneness. The red peels
are kisses, the stems are our bodies at sunset.

Our kisses, our bodies twine into the sunset
that bleeds away into the deepening dark.
A scalloping pattern of salmon until the blue
intonations are gutted with black. Little heart,
little baby—the swaddling clothes are embedded
with razors. Trust like a stable abandoned
the day after Christmas—a rental some truck
must pick up, ersatz Bethlehem star
losing luster in daylight. Snow will cover
the shape of our two bodies perfectly fitting
together. My fingers turn inward; the rays
they would send out get stuck in the knuckles.
The apples are well in the ground by December.
Their task is to somehow remember.

Their task is to somehow remember
the trees that produced and then shed
them. I can remember the sound
of your breathing, the soft of your ear
melting into my mouth, can remember
your hand on the arch of my spine
and the way love climbed over
the soft fence, the hard fence
to meet us where traffic seemed,
suddenly, to stop. That was lovely.
The dirt that sifts through cannot mute
the dank apples unraveling. Frost
cannot strangle their screaming.
I put my hand on your hand, like this—

like this hand on your hand as we slept,
like this hand on your arm as it held me.
We were two people falling down
into each other; we dug into each other,
the dirt of each other, the drug
of each other, the lock and the key
of each other. And love was the mother
nobody quite gets in this world; it made us
both children no longer regretting this world
and lovely—the traffic just stopped
and the stable was full of the blue
mother cradling her child. The livestock
they'd rented so docile. The steam of their breath
was suspended in floodlights, unending.

In unending floodlights, suspended,
the courthouse stood knowing its morning
would come. It was chalkwhite,
unflinching with right
and with wrong. Love of justice
and love are not ever the same. So
the baby turns into the monarch
and heart into brain, and the body
is led like the livestock up onto a ramp
that's not steep though it makes
all the difference from danger to safety.
Again, I choose safety, the core of the moon
breaking down in my fist, as I listlessly look
for a place to dispose it. My love,
the emotions go somewhere, they find—

## Because the Wind

seems more and more like the wails of guilty conscience
or a child's recriminations for being thrown into the world,
I stay inside.

Because it's a freight train slamming the neighbors apart,
we all stay inside, where fiber optics whisper consistently

while telephone lines fling like jump ropes—blossoming,
tightening—hearts in the air citing memorized songs;
in here, the hearts burrow

and tunnel through binary sinuses, blind snouts are pointing;
somewhere in Greece, a man is so lonely he photographs roses
and sends them

to where he imagines a woman must be. The wind peels
the prayer-banners off of the trunks of the trees that withstand
what we will not

withstand. Someone walks in her sleep in Australia; her teeth
are the clatter of keyboards. We do not need to sleep anymore
to have dreams.

I am watering roses in Crete while my continent's battered
by some old Atlantic resentment. The wind is a woman
who will not stay

quiet, a man who just will not stay put. Inside, the screens
watch us. They hope we will teach them our natures.
If the wind is an echo

of love, I can't hear, staring into this wade-pool tonight.

# A Local Joan of Arc,

stunned by sinlessness,
walks a country road past midnight.

Voices say God set the curtains on fire
that she might go forth, pull the animals out
of the brush on both sides of the road
and raise armies of them—opossum,
raccoon, groundhog, all the smaller ones
fed to the fierce tires, the mean grilles
of pick-up trucks, boys whose veins throb
with whatever they're using tonight.

Not far now: the walls of the city, lit up
perpetual twenty-four-seven—
the fortress—the place for reclaiming,
for cigarettes, sentries of gas pumps,
sweet and sour relics,
warm unblinking urns.

The animals move in her pockets, her armor.
She's never known man; if she has, she's
stood off from their pumping
and dogged but brief
ruminations.

For there is a king that she needs
to restore. Some have called him her father,
but that is impossible; that man's in jail.
But the man who put the needle in her arm
that first night, he spoke of his plan
for a peaceable kingdom.

By dawn, she is waiting, with just a few others,
for the sun-colored juice that tames the small
animals—noblest cause there can be.

# The Rain [Mainly] Falls

Against the red brick wall the fading grapevines have a grammar
of their own, half-born purple punctuation, frayed syntactic coughs.

[Manifesting:
Does that mean] our needs enliven empty form?

Last night the yellow echo chamber, moon-to-moon, confirmed
belief that all we ever have remaining is one day, if we're

honest
with ourselves. In less than two hours, roiling in the swamps
of their own glands, the people in the room morphed into every

living creature, then, in human form again, rolled from the shells
of their own corpses into fetal balls, plugged into lotus leaves

like batteries, stood, considered mountains, and went home.

[Intimacy:
Does that mean?] we share the same skull-cave at times, but scrawl

on separate sides of it. My tall and charcoal declarations, your
pips spelling out *hit / no-hit*. The steps beyond the lips of this

thick urn are merely Man domesticating Wolf again, the wolf
in the form of a cotton-ball, the wolf in the form of a roan Irish

skein unraveling in all directions but the leash. [Empiricism:

put this to the test and] it will sure enough dissolve. Yet,
I can't imagine anything more real than your rough palm

on my breast. So many insects come equipped with armor
though we figure as the smart ones when the light throws

up our shadows on the wall. [Projection: God,] the father
who forgets your middle name, the mother who, right

after parturition, sets the bundle gently on the curb and goes
about her business. When we part the curtains of our rented

security, the mastodons collecting garbage roar, the morning
is the very essence of denial, always has been for, however

raucous was the thing that came before, it's [Presto:
gone]. Carve it into wall or skin, or float it onto fiber.

## Camel Pose (Ustasana)

I felt like a hood ornament,
                              nude
                    like that; there
              must have been a glare
I doubt they would have
          seen as beautiful.
                    Knees planted for
                          the twenty-minute
              pose, my hands
like wrenches on
          my heels, my head an
                    afterthought and hair
                          a vine that sought
          the ground behind me,
I heard each scratch
          of every pencil, saw
                    the clockface upside-
                          down.  In camel,
              blood drained
through the C-curve
          of my neck to my
                    skull, steeping all my fears
                          till they dissolved
because now I was nothing
          but a body—good or bad—
                    and it was something
                          they could draw—
              it had mass; it was not
filthy.  Blemished, but
          the charcoal arcs in pebbly
                    rasps could trace it.  As
                          gravity revised
          my face, I drew in
breath from below &
          above me, breaths
                    that grazed my tailbone,
                          which was still

                    in place, while all my back
departed for another kind of stack
              in which each disk was re-
                        acquainted but with
                                distance (like
                  the spill of a suspension
bridge, or old love brought to new).


The camel and my body—
white and factual
              inside the bright—
                        could never be alike but
                                in diaphanous
                  intensity as lights
and sun bear down and in the
              spine a strange
                        endurance stores itself.
                                When I had lost
              all feeling and become
abstract, the timer shrieked, I lurched
              toward that mirage—
                        my body standing
              on two legs.

## Sometimes, Standing Still

is anaphora.
Standing still, one sees the clouds are moving
and the cliff is just an underbite
shoveling water to sky into water and then
standing still is a misty religion—
wishes and birds on the statues alight.

Sometimes, standing still is a mountain, one
of the earth's many goosebumps. Straight up
like a meerkat or hairs on a forearm,
we stand 'til the wind or exhaust beats us down.

Standing still
is anathema inside the city stripped clean
of its gold, where finding a living means
*making the right moves*, people on platforms
so full of the prospect of transit
they're swallowed in clattering wings.

Love amasses in stasis, content
with its form, despite trinkets and satellites
blinking; the moon, the earth's spinster
great-aunt, atomizes affection in
outdated perfumes of light.

You are part of me, all of me, valley or
something that lives on the sad side,
a bridge I can't cross.

Some days, love puts a uniform on, goes
to work, or to Whom It May Concern
in a dull yellow envelope. I say I'm seeking
out its face in the long time-card queue
but only trace my old excrescences
                              looking for you.

❧

If you'd only stand still,
you could own the left margin and
start every sentence,
could push your cart through the fluorescent
waxed aisles and be plowing a medieval field
at the same time, the sun's path pulling you
as you push, a balancing
that makes it seem
you're always only where you are.

❧

And when crushing fatigue creeps over the estate,
we could trade the mask of vex for beatific
where the margin finally crowns and is the center.

**Warrior II, Or "always be kind, for everyone you meet is fighting a great battle."**

Stand up.

Drop fruit. Wait for the seeds to make love to their allotment of ground.

As they rise, feel their pull from every side. Forget you once had angles, let

your head engulf the rest of you. *I draw the arm from eight points of view of which*

*three are from the outside, three are from the inside, one is from behind and one is*
                                                                *from in front*

If your arms extend into a spear, diameter of some great sphere inside which lives a
                                                                          warrior,

you will become disarmed, your gonads & guts inside a cup that's tipped just
                                                                    slightly up.

Ages pass, and then some bodybuilder dusts off old DaVinci sketches, dreams

a slow rotation of the torso inside acapella space, and builds a Web site.

Every angle is a curve if you can push it to its end and then

a little more. Nothing will break inside this space. Your gaze

a gift you carry just in case you're empty-handed: something good

to give a neutral spot above your fingertips, no strings attached,

no charcoal sighs of who owes whom or why it might be like this.

Retire the story of the Amazons hacking off one breast;

hesitate to break the trance, to consciously embrace the Philo quote.

It's a beautiful notion, though the attribution doesn't have legs.

The important thing is to make the move from spear to sphere as quietly as possible.

IV.

# Child's Pose (balasana)

A way of hitting back. One wave
the dreaded belt, sailing backward,
jerking forward, striking skin.
Large tides in which a small soul
swims. The child posed as a mouse
stunned into temporary death
until the predator forgets.

The child posed as a house of cold,
ungiving rafters. All alone, the child
is architect of hunger; face in shadow,
knees, feet, forehead touch the floor.
A small soul's scattered breath
and heartbeat echo, sounding out
the home inside the house.
A way of getting back—

the heels exposed, the unprotected soles—
bulbs of daffodils in snow.

# The Bow (dhanurasana)

I have nothing to do with Cupid or Fenimore Cooper or Diana
or Artemis or my brother Bob and his son in the ochre woods
looking out for ochre deer. I am more like a pair of rocking-chair
runners with a loose crossbar that, every so often, pops out
of the dowel—not disastrously—just enough to make me sure
I'm not a bow but a person whose only contact with the earth is
the bottom of her belly as her body locks its limbs and lifts away.

If arrows are intentions, God, I think I have too many.
They fly out in all directions. Just last week, I rocked
Keely's baby in my arms, and it was working, he was calming,
all his weight was molded to my chest, his breathing whittled
down to little pulls on the bottle's nipple. But the chair
was moving closer to the wall, and when the chairback hit the wall,
                                   I braced myself for the ragged wail.

If we only had one arrow, only got to use one arrow, would it land
where it should—between two things already cleft in two,
like my shoulder blades that nearly touch
when I reach back and grasp my ankles tight?

# Yoga for Housewives

In the book my mother bought in 1972, splayed over 50-odd black and white pages: a blonde maiden tower in Danskin and leotards, hipper than *The Mod Squad's* Peggy Lipton. Her morphing form and the narrating author taught my mom yoga, which she then taught me.

It's still in print today; we call it Yoga For Housewives. The plates re-inked so many times that, if you squint, they might be carbon dating samples or an illustrated Chaucer Kama Sutra titled *Fifty Ways to Cuckold Your Hubby*.

In Figure 19A, for instance, just before the model does her seated forward bend, just before the Lipton-chicken-soup-haired woman folds in two, she could easily be interrupted by Jack Lalanne and made to walk on her haunches across the plain of wall to wall shag carpeting, arms crossed, legs straight, singing the ancient chant against all chicken fat.

I use it still, to offset the hardcore Iyengar book—the best of both worlds, really, wrist articulation with no pressure to be celibate; hymen-busting stretches dictated in that dialect of condescension women learned to take as well-intentioned:

*Yoga as a way to not Let Yourself Go. Yoga as alternative to valium or the torrid aphasia of afternoon sex with local workmen. Yoga can spare you that sad divorcée's walk from telephone to bathroom mirror over and over, a slippered bassline to the cry of "Why, God, why!" and sundry other bitter bromides. Yoga is much more than just a sequence of asanas. You can, i.e., perform most household chores as yoga.*

*For instance, when you set the table, here's a chance to align your clavicle with the china dish held just below your bust, keeping them parallel as you lower it to the linen lotus surface. Or, imagine, when cleaning the shower, that you coil up and down, brush in hand, a spiralling waterfall from bottom to top and back again, wringing out the soap scum like bad thoughts.*

*The washing machine is the harvest moon, pregnant with shirts free of ring-around-the-collar. As you watch it toss and throb the clothes to perfect cleanliness, pretend that porthole full of suds is your very own cervix! Close your eyes. The day is long.*

# The Debtor Yogini

The debtor yogini lies in corpse pose at the guru's command. She pays debt or plays dead, her vital signs compounded daily. Lights down low, the carpet sighs in the soul cemetery. The guru murmurs thought away and breath rolls in and out—the tide. The tithe to the guru $10 a week. Feet hip-width apart, arms a few inches from her side, the debtor yogini pretends to believe it is only the present that matters.

Idea is to generate sun in the stomach. We are all units of the sun meeting sun. Stretch up, bend forward, lips kissing your shins. How many balance transfers can she do before her head aches with fluorescence? Is Citibank the sun? Is it happy to see me?

In plank pose, the yogini's a blank check—push-up pose, lowered to an impossible hovering just inches from the floor (vicious little gator arms; mud of knowing and avoidance, twenty years inside the swamp of getandspend).

A nervous squirrel crosses the lawn beyond the vault of *savasana*; at the same moment, another creditor deposits a message in her box, and she's pregnant with fear, she thinks, but corpses mustn't think until they rise from the dead at the end of the practice.

Flat on the floor, the yogini would rather be a cobra. The universe grants her a solid gold spine; she can rise from the swamp for an unblinking view of the far wall. Not a ledger at all.

## Bridge (kamdharasana)

> *Under thy shadow by the piers I waited;*
> *Only in darkness is thy shadow clear.*
> — Hart Crane, "To Brooklyn Bridge"

The water we knew once with all of our skin

                     is what lifts you, though you think—

your hands on the floor under-

            pinning your shoulders,

                 your heels anchored

there, near your buttocks —think your limbs are the pylons, the forces

that make water safe again, are the laborers

                 holding their breath

                    long enough to forget

how their wages can't stretch from bank to bank. How they bend over

backwards,

       say the money-mantras,

               give palms, heels, the balls

of their feet to the New World (to lift themselves up). Or the shadow below

is what lifts you, the tender trail of hopes

        that assemble the spine—

             hopes stored up on hard chairs

further inland, lined up and waiting for the patience to pay off.

             *Don't hold your breath.* The head

       lolls back at the end of the shift,

    a tulip on its last day, sun sliding down from the sky; it will rise

from the pallet

       it set in. Each side of the bridge is beginning

                and end—

# Forward Bend (paschimottanasana)

*One does not feel any weight on the back in correct Paschimottanasana.*
—B.K.S. Iyengar, *Light on Yoga*

I surrender to an avalanche of paper woes,
fold like paper, head aspiring to the toes.

I surrender to the days and nights of solitude,
my ribcage on my thighs—a nude
in charcoal, crude initial, husk, a shell—

I surrender to those who do not wish me well,
to those who would stand on my wide, open back.

My east surrenders to my west: sun is setting,
houses, faces, facts forgotten;
the day dissolves into skin-creases.
Chin against the shin—long razor-bone;
breasts on kneecap—rainclouds, stones.

Surrender to the time the body measures
and the time that measured breath refers to

far beyond the body. My north
and my south have never known

each other's worth; I fold the map.

## Ghazal: Tree Pose (vrksasana)

The trees are always watching everything that moves.
It's not the wings of birds but what they sing that moves.

It's not the scurry of the squirrel on the forest floor.
The trees can only see inside their ring what moves.

The clouds are traveling this evening, scraping canopies.
Can't you hear how all your leafy fingers move?

Do you feel how your roots chew up the past & make it new?
Your feet have not forgotten: That which lingers, moves.

Your trunk is watching, listening, and breathing through
the wavering steeple where the wheeling bats move.

Something's leaning hard on something else tonight,
a flat foot on a thigh until the slingshot moves.

I always thought that balance was a work of will,
but I fall out of tree pose most by trying not to move.

Bones and wood make chapels stand, cathedrals reach.
The nave is in the navel that my breathing moves.

There isn't any thing that watches harder than the trees.
The gargoyles hunker down and wait for wings to move.

## The Plough (halasana)

the crucifix folds          the crucifix *can fold*
arms meld to a fulcrum      hips and legs lift
until head and toes          meet on the ground

a dozen daily wars          are transformed
*into ploughshares*          where the chin
meets the chest            the mouth kisses
                 the heart

where the crown of the head    eases out
                            of the thorns

Intestines: above           restless organs: above
      Vena cava,
pubic bone warm          as the cupola eye
        of a fetus.

The spine is the furrow the plough pulls from earth
the spine is the teeth of the plough, moving backwards
from Calvary, that whole sad progress rewound.

Different way, different truth, different life.
Nobody's jackknife. Grapes before vinegar.
Dirt before dust. The torso an arbor, the blessing,
the shade of your breathing—

      Live there,

               if you can.

## Downward Facing Dog (adho mukha svanasana)

The tailbone: a steeple for this church of one. The head
                                    hangs heavy,
crown toward the floor, and the arms stretch out until
                                    the radical fingers just barely
hold their ground. Arms so numb they disappear.
Which is how they grow stronger.

❧

*What doesn't kill you makes you stronger*, a mother tells her little girl in
bed on the makeshift cot, dot in the vast domed stadium. Stuffed
animals float through the flooded city, miles from this encampment of
thousands, this patchwork quilt of temporary lives, an inverse sky
whose stars have lost their course. Where is the plush dog that always
broke her fall to sleep?  How much toxic water could it hold before it
sank? Arms gone numb from flailing at the choppers coming through
the clouds. A senator blames the people who stayed behind. *Survival of
the fittest*, chides old Noah, with his nuts and bolts and information.
*Crush the weak*, the Humvees on the street declare. There's whooping
down the block. I guess our football team is winning.

❧

The *asanas*, Iyengar says, *should be done in a clean airy place, free from
insects and noise.*

❧

When the heart's above the head, another kind of blood
is filtered through the body. When the head is underneath
the heart, the tide. When the heart is bearing down like
giving birth to some new baby-brain whose only real
opinion is there's pleasure and there's pain—is God?

Each posture some kind of creature. Each minute
some kind of creature. Each creature is some sort
of time but not waiting. A dog in a stretch is both here
and not there, an ellipsis from sleeping to waking,
a person unmaking the noise, infestation of self. Is

pleasure and pain a kind of weather? Does the dog?
And if it doesn't heed the weather, isn't *under the*
*weather* as the weather rages on and has its way,
what does the dog? Or is the dog the stretch itself
and not the body that could bark and growl if only

it could see a city under water,
under a lid that the leaders don't lift
until it's too late. In the beginning,
keep the eyes open. Then you will know
*what you are doing and where you go wrong—*

❧

*And so many of the people in the arena here, you know, were*
*underprivileged anyway, so this—is working very well for them.*

---

*While performing asanas, the student's body assumes numerous forms*
*of life found in creation—from the lowliest insect to the most perfect*
*sage—and he learns that in all these there breathes the same Universal*
*Spirit—the spirit of God.*

❧

When my head touches the floor, I will know I am no
one. Until then, I lean into gravity's musk-heavy chest.

August the dog days have ended. Up north, we had rain,
some high winds; that was all. The locusts are my night-

time arena; they peel all my certainties off. The dogs
they use to locate bodies in the Gulf Coast mud and rubble

whimper when they find one. Their forelegs flat out
on the injured ground, they raise their behinds,

and they whimper.

*September 2005*

## The Lotus (padma)

They also serve who sit and wait        *they sit*    *they serve*    *they wait*

T H E Y  B R A I D  T H E I R  L E G S    they pray   they mountain-pose

they sink their tailbones into dirt to germinate  (or sit and sew and in so
doing
also serve  or so said Homer  then said Milton  then said Alice Dunbar-Nelson;
others like my mother send off shoots and shoots of prayer and I have felt them
all around me tickling my sitting skin).  O R

you can cut the braided ends by standing up and doing something  like a knife
or saying something—forming words, a human vice:
it hurts too much  to know your love is in Iraq inside a warzone we created
headphones helmeting his skull to drown out language
*to make the bass louder / than the mortar's thump* –

T O  C A R V E  T H E  H A R D  W O R D S  O N T O  S L A T E

They issued legs, they didn't say what they were for in times like this

to stand and rage and not to wait, or vegetate inside a *perfect knot of peace*

blood vessels blooming pink above *the murky mudchoked water* .

*For Shannon Spies and Brian Scullion*

# The Crow (bakasana)

These are the sticks you have
to stand on, these are
the issues you keep pulling out
with your plum-colored
thumb—nothing shiny
about them. Radius,
ulna and humerus;
haglike the
carpals
pretend
to hold
on.

Unbelievably topheavy, all of it,
just like dinosaurs in pictures
always on the brink of
toppling over. We agree
that birds are our dinosaurs, irony
being that things that can fly
seem unable to stand.

The couple
flies into each other,
a symmetry
beak to beak
(oh you should envy them,
trying again and again
on your weak twigs
to be the crow,
*come into* crow, or as some
yogis say, *flying into* it).

Backbending into the past is my forté
(my frown is a smile upside-
down),
but falling nose-first into
future, the outcome of dinosaurs
being the irony standing
and  barely a couple
again and again
on the brink

unbelievably?

# The Crow, Sobering

There is so much to know about the
crow, whose address is a nest
on a nautical trope, or is only
its two legs, ballasted by wings;
pinned back, forgetting everything,
they tip it toward the future,

an entity prophesied by futuristic
shrieks of the many, throwing off the
bearings of everything
(such sounds never come from a nest)
until the moment is a martinet with wings,
and latitudes and longitudes are only

lonely. With a bottle, you can have your own lee-
ward listing on liquid, not the future
which is air on which wings
might be cut. When you list the
weight that holds you here's a nest
comprising everything.

Crows in dark bars: Everything
is deferred until all of it seems only
yesterday and not a minute further.
I would love to crawl into your nest
and check these tarry, heavy wings
at the door! To begin each sentence, "The"

"The" "The" "The" "The" "The" "The"
and definitely not finish anything
until the big vinyl wingback swings
back into sleep, an only
deeper, darker nest.
As for futures,

further the nest:
nothing, only wings.

# Hips Don't Lie (eka pada rajakapotasana)

They are handles, both sides of the basket—cradles to old
phone receivers sputtering messages:

*You're breaking up*

(as if something so vital could ever be replaced).

Toward the end of my practice, I fold like a pigeon asleep
in the shadows of the darkening studio. The hips are where
some people store their emotion: that's why they squawk
in this pose. There's a difference between pain and discomfort.
For pain, you back off; discomfort, breathe into it
and let the joints open, sad lockets holding strands of loss
so remote that only the dark insides remember,

and hips don't lie, they are

parentheses around what is essential—solar plexus, *dan tien,*
the core caught up in *uddiyana bandha*—sober stones
weighing down every splay-winged messenger—

Marjorie's husband and Raymond's mother and Joseph's
cycling accident, and this one and that one—forever
the hips are discarded, replaced, they are blips on the screen
of our presence. Hinged and contingent. Let them open
at long last, and listen to those babies wail.

## Ichthus / Monkey Tails

I like the simian way we sleep, back to back, our spines stringy siblings,
our tailbones two knobs to two doors that have opened and closed to
the burnt orange pull of the earth. If I only had a tail, it would cross
over yours to make a fish-shape, the ichthus that stands for
                         *God-so-loved-the-world.* Love the worlds we roll
            over,
the worn sheets, the ships, fishes, history. When I crown you king,
I get a crown too because time curves and space curves and I
                         curve into you. There are six broken lines, one
            completely off the map;
still, these limbs begin again! I love the fur on all four of our arms.
We may have left some trees behind still golden in their meaning,
brown batik of dungish leaves.
                         Is it always more dense at the bottom
yet bright at the top, and is this why the dying begins right away,
a slow shading, the arm of duration first raked, then furry, then sleeved?
            Each time we devolve, I swing out for forever, burn rings
            around all
of your breathing.   When I look down, I am clinging like a sore cloth,
            but when I look up, there's no need.


after Patricia Bellan-Gillen's serigraph, *Premonition/Relocation*

# Raymond's Pantoum

My love has found a way
to pull green beans
from thin topsoil:
velvet martian fingers.

To pull beans
from rented yard-space,
he spreads his fingers.
I can feel them

in my yard space
breaking clods of dirt,
can feel them
taking me to Mars

by breaking clouds of dirt
until my reds all glow.
He's taken me so far
I do not know myself

until my reds all glow.
I don't know what to say;
I do not know myself,
but walk about all day

not knowing what to say
except there's sun, there's earth
to walk upon all day,
and I'm stem stretching

between sun and earth,
night and day. To put
down roots in a rootless world,
my love has found a way.

## Traum Song

Life is painful, sad, and methodical.
I must not say that.
Ever to confess
(remember when I thought I was
a lioness that night in May
and could have made six babies?)
Facts are thinner recourses.
Born: day month year
Died: day month year
Nothing new here people!!!
Just two doors or one
that swings two ways.

I've a pound of flounder in the fridge,
some lemon and organic butter,
a seep of parsley in the backyard snow,
two cats, a grown child & a love companion
with a weak aortic valve.
My fear is ticking too tall for the shelf
so I bend ninety minutes to the floor,
the guru streaming in through my PC
telling me the shape I'm in.

The light in me, the light in me
Christ I want it to
see the light in you—

## Rather than leaving the key under the mat,

I've left the clatter in my skull. On any given day,
the door will swing open on voice recognition:

good luck picking out the voice that unlocks it,
which is to say my soul is a clementine

and has to be enjoyed as a whole case of clementines,
and if you can't make that commitment in these times

of parceled generosities and tendencies toward retail,
I understand. But you should know the house is ripe

for burglary: a galaxy of pillbugs under sudden
lifted rock; a cabinet whose bric à brac's refractory

to allegory. Which is to say my soul would like
to be a clementine, those little mouths

so sweetly sewn into a center that seems hand-
stitched like the pages of the book perhaps this is.

See the Welcome on the mat? It's made of sentience
and sentiment and artificial dyes—good clatter-

cover, if I do say so myself—but I don't, because
you owe me nothing, least of all the explanation

I owe you. Justifications are gravy after all our arms
and legs have gone through, juice of sunlight pulped

to rain that streaks the glassy eyes of every storey.
Still, if the throat can clear itself to hold a note,

I hope the antlers of the sun are mounted in
my darkest room like stoic clothespins.

# Notes

"The Locust: A Foundational Narrative": In yoga, the locust, or *salabhasana*, is a mild backbend done lying face down and lifting legs, arm, head, and chest from the ground.

The italicized reference to Roberto Clemente's neck as "arrogant" comes from numerous accounts of his amazing career as a right-fielder for the Pittsburgh Pirates, which ended in a tragic airplane accident on New Year's Eve, 1972, when Clemente was carrying aid to Nicaragua to help the earthquake victims there. For instance, Pittsburgh sportswriter Phil Musick wrote that Clemente was "vain, often arrogant." As a fangirl growing up during this time, I sensed that the use of this adjective to describe Clemente often carried a racialized resentment in it, even if that was not always the intention.

B.K.S. Iyengar (1918-2014), who founded the Iyengar yoga practice in Pune, India, turned to yoga when he was young in order to strengthen his body following a series of illnesses. This practice has spread throughout the world, and he was important in helping to introduce yoga asana practice to the West.

"The Annunciation": In Tanner's painting of the New Testament account of the angel Gabriel's visitation of Mary, which led to her conception of Jesus Christ, the rug at the virgin's feet is slightly buckled, an interesting detail; there are numerous paintings of this scene, and many other poets, including Elizabeth Alexander and Mary Szybist, have been moved to write of them.

"Gin & Tonic": Bacchus, or Dionysius—the god of revelry and wine— is traditionally portrayed with a crown made of grape leaves.

"Minor Casualty, 2003": As a child of the sixties and the daughter of a policeman, I was acutely aware of, but insulated from, the 1968 riots that broke out following the assassination of Martin Luther King, Jr.; the largest riots occurred a couple of miles across the river from the predominantly white Pittsburgh neighborhood I was raised in.

"Rolling Rock Beer": The Mellon banking family owns extensive amounts of land and a country estate in the Laurel Highlands of Westmoreland County, Pennsylvania, about 50 miles southeast of Pittsburgh.

"Camel Pose": This pose, *ustasana,* is a kneeling backbend in which one works towards grabbing one's heels and raising chest to the sky.

"Warrior II, Or 'always be kind . . .'": The italicized quote in the body of the poem comes from Leonardo DaVinci's anatomy sketches; the quote in the title is frequently attributed to Philo of Alexandria, though that attribution has just as frequently been called into question.

"Child's Pose": This yoga asana, *balasana* in Sanskrit, is a resting pose in which one kneels and folds forward, placing the forehead on the ground; in practice, it is a posture assumed when one needs to take a time out and refocus on breathing.

"The Bow *(dhanurasana)*": The bow is a more intense "belly" backbend, often following the locust pose. As with the locust, one begins by lying facedown, then raising head, chest, legs, and arms; then the knees bend, and one grabs hold of the ankles or feet, creating a tense bowing and rocking of the spine and torso.

"Yoga for Housewives": I've changed the name of the book's title and author, but those who have used it will surely recognize it. Despite its dated condescension, it was one of my first yoga teachers, and I wore out at least one copy of it.

"The Debtor Yogini": *Savasana,* or corpse pose, is usually the posture that ends a yoga practice as final relaxation and integration of the various asanas, or postures, into the body. One lies on one's back, relaxing every muscle and bone.

The plank pose is called *chaturanga dandasana,* which means "four-limbed staff." It is a low-push up, with arms bent so that the upper arms are parallel with the sides of the torso; many of my teachers have referred to it as "alligator" posture. And the cobra posture is done from the facedown prone position: While keeping most of the body on the ground, one raises one's upper body as far as the spine will allow, mimicking the spread hood of the snake.

"Bridge": *Kamdharasana* is a backbend in which one lies on one's back, knees bent and feet flat on the floor, and raises the hips and pelvis while keeping the upper body on the ground.

"Forward Bend": The forward bend, or *paschimottanasana,* explored in this poem is a seated posture in which one bends forward from the waist, with the goal of extending the torso down to the legs and the head toward the feet. It is often referred to as the posture of surrender.

"Ghazal: Tree Pose": *Vrksasana* is a standing balance posture that involves pressing the sole of one foot against the inner thigh of the other leg; one can fold hands, prayer-style, against the sternum in this pose or raise arms up like the branches of a tree.

"The Plough": *Halasana* is one of the yoga inversions in which, lying on the back, one raises straight legs up over the head until the toes touch the ground. It is generally spelled "plow" in American English, but I've used the alternate spelling in order to evoke the Biblical notion of transforming swords into ploughshares, in line with the poem's numerous references to the crucifixion of Christ at Calvary and the possibility of reimagining it, as yoga inversions are often seen as opportunities to see things from a new perspective.

"Downward Facing Dog": Italicized quotes come from a statement made to the press by Barbara Bush shortly after Hurricane Katrina in 2005 and from B.K.S. Iyengar's *Light on Yoga.*

"The Lotus": This is the seated *padma* posture where legs are crossed in order to lock one into stillness; the poem collages lines and phrases from John Milton's Sonnet 19, Sir Philip Sidney's *Astrophil and Stella* XXXIX, Alice Dunbar-Nelson's "I Sit and I Sew," and from a chapbook by Brian Scullion, a young writer who completed a tour in Iraq in the early aughts.

"The Crow": *Bakasana* is an arm-balancing posture that has been a great struggle for me in my years of practice. In this pose, only one's flat palms are on the ground, since the knees rest on the upper triceps. As Baron Baptiste notes in *Journey Into Power*, the pose can literally bring the practitioner face-to-face with the fear of falling forward.

"Hips Don't Lie": The poem takes its title from the 2005 song by Shakira (feat. Wyclef Jean). *Dan tien* is a term used in tai chi and the martial arts to refer to the "energy center" of the body in the abdomen; I understand this be related to the yogic *uddiyana bandha,* or abdominal lock, in that the latter is an attempt to harness the energy of the former. The solar plexus, or core, is the hub in yoga, as it is in other mind-body practices.

"Ichthus / Monkey Tails": "Ichthus" is the Greek word for "fish." The *OED* defines it as "a stylized representation of a fish in profile, consisting of a pointed oval extended by two lines at one end (representing a tail), used as symbol for Jesus Christ." The ichthus is among us in the form of the "Jesus fish" many Christians display on their car bumpers; that fish is emended and given feet by those who support the idea of evolution. This poem engages that tension between religion and science.

"Traum Song": The poem is a loose recasting of John Berryman's *Dream Song* 14. "Traum" is a German word for "dream," and of course, the poem is associating the word with the idea and experience of trauma. The poem's closing lines are a vernacularized English translation of the Sanskrit greeting *namaste,* which is often said at the end of a yoga practice.

# Acknowledgments

A large portion of the yoga poems' process and evolution was made possible by an Individual Artist Fellowship in Poetry from the Pennsylvania Council on the Arts and by a generous anonymous Pittsburgh patron. Special thanks to A Room of One's Own Foundation and Michelle Aldredge for selecting "The Locust: A Foundational Narrative" for a 2012 Orlando Prize.

Many thanks to editors and publishers of the following publications in which some of these poems have first appeared:

- Journals: *The American Poetry Review, Bayou, Cimarron, Kestrel, The Los Angeles Review, Manor House Quarterly, Ninth Letter, Rufous City Review, Quiddity, TPQ Online, Weave,* and *Ghost Town.*

- Anthologies: *A Joyful Noise: The Autumn House Anthology of Spiritual Poetry* (Autumn House, Pittsburgh), *99 Poems for the 99 Percent* (99: The Press, San Francisco), *The Poetry of Yoga* 2 (Lulu. com/One Common Unity), *Voices from the Attic* (Carlow University Press, Pittsburgh), and *...and love...* (Jacar Press, Durham, NC).

- Chapbook: *Scatter, Feed* (Editor's Series 2.10, The Seven Kitchens Press, Lewisburg, PA, 2014).


Many thanks to my poetry readers, writing group comrades, supporters, and friends over the years including Julie Parson Nesbitt and John Crawford of West End Press, Ron Mohring of The Seven Kitchens Press, Judith Vollmer, Sharon F. McDermott, Barbara Edelman, Jeff Oaks, Beth Newborg, Toi Derricotte, Jenny Johnson, Jane McCreery, Rina Ferrarelli, Gail Ghai, Deborah and Jim Bogen, Lynn Emanuel, Joy Katz, Pam Goldman, John Schulman, Justin Vicari, Jane McCafferty, Nancy Koerbel, Lynn Giroux, Lynn Wagner, Mary Matejevich, Sandy Mitchell, Yona Harvey, Joe Ramsey, Brian Clements, Michael Wurster, Keely Bowers, and Geeta Kothari; to Ann Dernier and Kore Press for invaluable feedback; to Jan Beatty and the

Madwomen in the Attic; and to the University of Pittsburgh Department of English. I also want to thank those who have kept me going at all times, writing or not: The McGrath and Smith families, Cristina Smith Correnti, Raymond Frances, Robin Santhouse, Marcia Bronder Warren, Gloria Bronder Konwick, Frank Correnti, Lynn Conroy, Lisa Schwartz, and my yoga teachers, beginning with my mother and including Adrienne Totino, Kimberly Musial, and the many mighty instructors at Sean and Karen Conley's Amazing Yoga studios in Pittsburgh—bottoms up and namaste!